The Nature Club
Taking Flight

Edited by Emma Irving and Julie Mazur Tribe

A portion of the proceeds from the sale of this book will
benefit bird conservation in Nicaragua.

Library of Congress Cataloging-in-Publication Data is
available upon request.
ISBN 978-1-7329156-0-2 (paperback)
ISBN 978-1-7329156-5-7 (ebook)

First edition 2019

10 9 8 7 6 5 4 3 2 1

Wild Bear Press operates on the simple premise
that nature-based stories connect children with
the natural world and inspire them to protect it.

Visit us on the Web! www.natureclubbooks.com

The Nature Club
Taking Flight

Rachel Mazur

WILD BEAR
PRESS

For Wren, the little bird who
pulls my heartstrings
(in California)

and for Natalie and Shanti
(in Nicaragua)

1

"Hoohoohoohoo . . . hoo . . . hoo . . ."

Izzy Philips listened to the deep hooting of the great horned owl as she lay awake in her tent. The sound soothed her as she remembered the news her mom had shared only the day before. She twisted a strand of her long, dark hair as she imagined saying goodbye to her best friend, Brooke, at the end of summer, the two of them pinky promising to stay best friends forever.

When her eyes started to water, Izzy reminded herself that it was still three months away. She leaned over and whispered to her little brother, "Zack, are you awake?" The lump that was Zack in his sleeping bag didn't answer but simply rose and fell to the rhythm of his snores.

Checking her watch, she saw it was only five o'clock—too early to be awake, let alone wake anyone else. Izzy rolled over and reached under her pillow for her headlamp, notebook, and pen and started a letter to her pen pal, Miguel.

Dear Miguel,

I have horrible news. My mom got a job in Southern California and we have to move at the end of the summer. I love living in Greenley, California! In this little town, we are right in the Sierra Nevada and are surrounded by nature. When we move, I'll have to go to fifth grade in a new school in a big city, where they make the kids wear uniforms and give speeches. I can't talk in front of people!

And I can't leave Brooke—she's my best friend. And I can't leave my gymnastics class. After trying all year, I can finally almost do a back handspring. Mom said we'll come back and visit, but it won't be the same. I'm scared about moving. What if I don't make any new friends? How are you?
Your friend,
Izzy

Izzy sniffed and wiped her eyes with the back of her hand. Then she tucked her headlamp, notebook, and pen back under her pillow. "Don't worry, I'm sure we'll learn to like the big city," she said doubtfully to the sleeping lump next to her.

Finally, the first light of morning peeked through the tent. Izzy rolled onto her back and listened as the meadow came alive. First there was the *cheer-up, cheerily* of the robin and the *konk-ka-ree* of the red-winged blackbird. Next came the whistling and buzzing of warblers, flycatchers, and vireos. When the woodpeckers finally joined in, drumming on the trees outside her tent, Izzy sat up, wide awake.

She wiggled out of her warm sleeping bag and slipped on a cold pair of jeans and a worn-out sweatshirt. As she pulled her hair back into her standard ponytail, she whispered to her still-sleeping brother that she'd be back soon. She unzipped the tent, stepped outside to stretch, and walked down to where her yard ended and her beloved Green County Park began.

Izzy took a deep breath of the fresh morning air and looked around. In the meadow, the dew-covered grass and spider webs sparkled in the morning light. Surrounding it, the lush green of the trees was offset by a colorful cascade of flowers.

As Izzy took it all in, a bright-yellow bird darted through the willows. Izzy tiptoed closer until suddenly, the bird flew out of the willows and perched on a nearby branch. It was tiny, with a longish tail and a thin little beak, and it hopped quickly from branch to branch while chattering at her. "What are you hiding, little bird?" Izzy asked.

She pulled apart the willow branches to peek inside. There, at the base of one of the willows, was a tiny nest. It was made of dried leaves and moss and lined with fine grasses and what looked like deer hair. She leaned closer. Inside were five tiny eggs! They were creamy white and glossy, and ringed with a darker pattern at one end. Izzy watched the nest for a full minute before she realized one of the eggs was shaking.

2

Inside the egg, hidden from Izzy's curious gaze, a baby bird was getting ready to hatch. He took a big gulp of air, tensed his neck muscles, and slammed his beak against the shell again and again. *Wham! Bam! Whack!* He had grown an egg tooth on the end of his beak just for this moment, and it was proving its worth. A few more whacks and finally, *crack!* The bird then bashed his head against the opening until it was wide enough for him to wiggle through—and he was out!

For the first time in his short life, he felt the wind and sun on his wet skin. He couldn't fly, for he didn't yet have feathers, and he couldn't see since his eyes hadn't yet opened, but he could eat, and boy, was he hungry. He threw back his head, stretched his beak wide open, and demanded to be fed. "*Chirp, chirp, chirp!*"

The yellow mother bird heard her chick calling to her, but her path was blocked. She jumped about, anxiously waiting to return until the girl with the long brown ponytail finally left the area. Then the yellow bird flew straight to her baby and stuffed an insect into his throat. He gulped it down, but in a moment, his beak was back open. "*Chirp, chirp, chirp,*" he called out again as his mother flew off for more food.

Then one of the other eggs started to shake, and then another. One by one, the baby birds hatched out and started chirping. Soon, all five nestlings were sitting together in the nest with their beaks wide open, frantic to be fed.

As the mother worked, a second bird flew in and peered into the nest. He looked just like her, except the top of his head was black, making him look like he was wearing a little cap. Soon, both parents were working full time to feed the hungry babies. They worked constantly, flying off to find insects and returning quickly to stuff them down their babies' throats, and the babies still demanded more and more and more.

3

Izzy made it back to her tent just as Zack called out, "Izzy? Izzy! Where are you?"

"I'm right outside the tent," she replied. "You aren't going to believe what I just saw!"

"You left me here alone? Where'd you go?" Zack complained.

"Oh, come on! Don't be such a chicken. You were sleeping forever," Izzy said. "I went to see what a bird was doing in the willows and found its nest. I saw one of its babies hatch! Don't worry," she said. "I was never so far from the tent that I couldn't listen for you, and besides, Mom is right in the house."

"You saw a bird hatch out of its egg?" Zack asked, rubbing his eyes. "You are so lucky!"

"C'mon, I'll show you!"

It was Zack's turn to crawl out of his warm

sleeping bag. "Brrrr!" he yelled, fumbling to pull on his sweatshirt. Zack unzipped the tent, and out came his two dirty feet in flip-flops, followed by the rest of him—a grinning five-year-old with short, red hair sticking straight up and one arm wrapped around Otto, his stuffed penguin. He zipped the tent closed and off they went.

Almost immediately, Izzy spotted one of her schoolmates walking along the far side of the meadow. It was Tai, the new boy in her class. She recognized him by his ever-present cowboy hat. He had just moved to Green County from Nebraska, and Izzy hadn't talked to him yet. Actually, Izzy didn't talk to anyone at school except her friend Brooke—especially not boys. Izzy looked for something to hide behind, but it was too late.

"Hey there!" Tai called. "You're Izzy, right?"

"Yes," Izzy said quietly. "Hello." She put her head down and kept walking, but Tai stopped right in her path.

"What're you doing out here?" he asked. "And

so early!"

Who do you think you are? Izzy thought. *This is my spot.* But instead of saying that, she muttered, "We were camping. We live right there," and pointed to the house just beyond their green tent.

"No kidding," said Tai. "You must have one lucky penny!"

"What? I mean, yes, we are lucky. Well, uh, why are *you* here?" Izzy asked. She looked up at Tai, noticing for the first time the friendly smile and vivid dark eyes that were usually hidden under his hat.

"My dad studies birds. He's settin' up a bird-banding station like the one he had in Nebraska. He always brings me along—even when he has to shake me out of bed to get me goin'."

"Can't you stay with your mom?" asked Izzy.

"My parents split before we moved here," Tai answered, kicking the dirt with his boot. "My mom still lives in Nebraska."

"Oh," said Izzy, twisting her hair. "Do you miss

your mom?"

Zack tugged on Izzy's shirt. "C'mon, Izzy. Let's go," he whispered. But now Izzy was focused on what Tai had to say.

"Yeah, I miss her a lot," Tai said quietly. He looked into the distance for a few seconds.

"We live with just our mom," Izzy said. "Our dad . . . our dad died a few years ago, right after our little brother, Carson, was born. I miss him a lot, too."

"Oh, I'm sorry," Tai said and kicked the dirt some more.

Izzy tried to think of something else to say. "Sooo . . . um, do you help your dad band birds?"

"I sure do," Tai answered, perking up. "How 'bout you come along sometime?"

"That sounds great!" replied Izzy, even though she didn't know what banding was and was too shy to ask.

Zack poked Izzy. "I wanna do it, too."

"Um, well, I don't know," Izzy said. She turned to Tai. "Can my brother come, too?"

"Heck yes, he can come," Tai answered. "He can even bring that penguin of his." He looked down at Zack and added, "But tell your penguin that since he's a bird, he just might get banded."

With wide eyes, Zack clutched Otto tightly to his chest.

Tai grinned. "Don't worry, kid. Banding won't hurt a bit." He bent over to pick a long piece of grass to chew on and turned to Izzy. "Dad will be banding here in a couple weeks. I sure hope you come."

"Me too. Thanks for inviting us," Izzy replied. It was hard to believe just a few minutes ago she'd been trying to avoid Tai. She felt so mixed up about the whole thing she forgot all about the nest and took Zack back to the tent to pack up.

4

The next couple weeks were busy at Izzy and Zack's house. In addition to school, they helped their mom start preparing for their move. That meant going through everything they owned and then holding a garage sale to get rid of the extra stuff. They also spent a lot of time taking care of their two-year-old brother, Carson, while their mom "arranged things" for the move.

On the second weekend in May, their mom took a trip to Southern California to meet with her new boss and find the family a place to live. While she was gone, Izzy, Zack, and Carson stayed with their Grandma Pearl, who was their mom's mom and lived just a few blocks away.

Izzy loved Grandma Pearl's house. It was cool in the summer and warm in the winter and smelled like lavender. Colorful homemade quilts brightened all the beds, and more were piled on the couch for when they watched movies. Outside, there was a huge flower garden decorated with quirky metal statues of gnomes and fairies and a trampoline she'd bought just for their visits.

Of course, the best part of Grandma Pearl's house was Grandma Pearl. She was smart, funny, a great listener, and a great storyteller. When Izzy begged, Grandma Pearl told stories about being the first girl to join her high school's ice hockey team and one of the first three women to get a college degree in physics.

Her stories were full of adventure, and regardless of whether she was telling them about something scary or exciting, they were always hilarious. Grandma Pearl always ended her stories by telling the kids they could achieve great things if they believed in themselves.

On Izzy, Zack, and Carson's second day at Grandma Pearl's, they walked back to their own house to get the mail. Zack skipped ahead while

Grandma Pearl pushed Carson in his stroller. Izzy quietly dragged behind. All she could think about was how much she would miss their neighborhood, Grandma Pearl, Brooke, and Green County Park. Her eyes teared up again. It just wasn't fair that they had to move. She looked up and saw Grandma Pearl waiting for her to catch up, a look of concern on her face. They walked in silence for a few minutes.

"Your mom is so excited about making things better for you and your brothers," Grandma Pearl said. "How are you feeling about the move?"

Izzy burst into tears. "How am I feeling? Awful! I love it here! Why do we have to move? What if I hate it there? I don't want to leave!"

Grandma Pearl stopped and hugged her tightly. Tears streamed down Izzy's face. Grandma Pearl let her cry, whispering, "I love you, little Bean."

After a few minutes, Izzy's sobs slowed down. She breathed in her grandma's sweet lavender scent and hugged her even more tightly.

Grandma Pearl bent down and looked deeply into Izzy's eyes. "You are stronger than you think," she said. "Trust yourself and be brave. This seems hard now, but you'll be just fine."

Izzy took a deep breath and smiled at her grandma. Somehow, Grandma Pearl always knew how to make things better. The two of them started walking again, finally catching up to Zack. "You two took *forever*!" he shouted. Izzy laughed. Her worries were far from gone, but maybe they could wait until tomorrow.

"Race you to the mailbox!" Grandma Pearl shouted as she ran ahead with Carson in the stroller.

When they reached the mailbox, they were all panting and laughing. Zack reached in and pulled out a single envelope. "Izzy! It's for you!" he yelled, waving it at her. It was a reply from her pen pal, Miguel. Izzy sat down and tore it open.

Querida Izzy,

I am sorry to hear you will move. I have lived my whole life in one place and don't know what it's like to move. If only you were moving to Nicaragua, we could do things together. You know, there are birds that migrate between your country and mine. Do you know about these birds? They are born up in your country and then fly south to spend the fall and winter down in mine. In the spring, they fly back north to spend the spring and summer back up near you. They go back and forth like that for their whole lives.

If I could, I'd fly up and visit you in your new home, even if it meant migrating north in the fall! But you would need to play soccer with me. Most people in Nicaragua play baseball, but I love soccer. My team is the Tiburones—that means sharks. I play center midfielder. Anyway, you will be fine! I think you will have a big adventure. And hey, you are supposed to be writing me in Spanish!

Saludos,

Miguel

Izzy smiled. Back at the beginning of third grade, everyone in her Spanish class had been assigned a pen pal. It was now a year and a half later—they were almost done with fourth grade—and Izzy and Miguel were still writing to each other.

But Miguel was right, she had been lazy and had been writing in English. Izzy twisted her hair and added "write to Miguel in Spanish" to her list of worries for tomorrow.

5

Meanwhile, back in the willows, the two yellow birds made trip after trip to bring food to their noisy nestlings. The chicks stopped demanding food only when they were asleep at night. But as soon as they woke, "Chirp, chirp, chirp," it started again. It went on like that for ten days. But the parents' hard work paid off. The nestlings fattened up and their first set of feathers grew in.

Then, on the eleventh day, they could no longer fit in their nest. It was time for them to leave—to graduate from nestlings to fledglings. They couldn't yet fly, but the nest was close to the ground. The bird that had hatched first hopped onto the rim of the nest and peeked over the edge. One of his sisters raced past him and jumped out. "Cheep, cheep!" She called as she landed on her side. Then another sister jumped, and then a brother.

The three little balls of fluff chirped and peeped while trying to get back onto their feet. The first-hatched bird jumped next, managing to land upright, but not for long. "Cheep, cheep, cheep!" The last brother jumped and crashed into the others, which made all five balls of fluff roll around in a general panic with lots of chirping and fluttering about.

A fox heard the commotion and crept up close. He saw there weren't just one or two, but five tasty little birds to eat and bared his teeth in anticipation. The first-hatched bird, the one that had finally managed to get back on his feet, saw those big teeth—and above them, the two large eyes that were watching him intently. Instinctively, he froze and so did his siblings. But it was too late. The fox had seen them and wasn't about to leave without his lunch.

As the fox flexed his muscles to spring forward onto his prey, the mother bird flew down between the fox and her nestlings. She began to flutter about on the ground as if she had a broken wing, which caught the fox's attention. An adult bird would make for better eating than a handful of small ones.

But just as he tried to pounce on her, the mother bird flew to a high branch and chattered at him. The fox whirled back to snatch the fledglings, but they were gone, safely hidden among the willows. With his head hanging low, the fox slunk off. He had been tricked.

After that near-death experience, the first-hatched bird needed to learn to fly. After a few practice flights, he flew all the way to a nearby branch. As he flew, he felt the freedom of having nothing but air beneath his wings. He rested for a moment and then took off again. But just a few seconds into his second flight, that feeling of freedom disappeared. It felt like he was staying in one place. He realized he *was* staying in one place—he was stuck in a net!

He fluttered about frantically, but found the more he moved, the more stuck he became, so he lay still. Soon another bird flew into the net above him and then two more flew into the net below him. They also struggled at first and then gave up to wait. But for what? They didn't know.

6

That same morning, there was a lot of excitement at Izzy and Zack's house. The kids were back from staying at Grandma Pearl's, and today was the day they would meet Tai to go banding. Izzy's best friend Brooke was coming along, too, and she had stayed overnight so they could all wake up early.

Zack woke up first and yelled, "Banding time!" Brooke leaped out of bed and changed into purple shorts and a rainbow top, slipping a sparkly headband into her curly black hair. It was tougher to get Izzy up. She'd hardly slept at all because she was excited about the banding and also a little nervous. Zack and Brooke had to turn on all the lights and jump on her bed to get her up.

The three kids headed downstairs together to find something to eat for breakfast. In the kitchen, they found Izzy's mom, who had already made pancakes for everyone. "Morning, Mrs. Philips!" said a bright-eyed Brooke, followed by Izzy's sleepy, "Hi Mom." Zack just smiled while his mom greeted him with a kiss on the head.

The three kids gobbled up the entire stack of pancakes, gave Mrs. Philips a group hug, and rushed out of the house.

When the kids got to the designated meeting place at the biggest oak tree, they saw Tai there with two men. One sipped coffee from a thermos and, like Tai, wore a cowboy hat. The other wore glasses, had curly brown hair poking out from under a gray knit cap, and wrote notes on a clipboard.

Brooke strode right up with a big smile. "We're here!" she announced. Izzy had already introduced Brooke, who was a year younger, to Tai in the school cafeteria.

Izzy, bringing up the rear, blushed, her nervous stomach twisting in knots.

"Hey there!" Tai said with an easy grin that helped Izzy relax.

"Hi Tai," she said softly.

"This is my dad," he said, pointing to the man with the cowboy hat.

"Hi kids," the man said, putting down his coffee and revealing a thick, black mustache. "I'm Mr. Davis. Glad you could come."

"Hi Mr. Davis," said the kids at the same time.

"And this here is Mr. Harris," he continued, pointing to his partner.

"Hi Mr. Harris," the kids said at the same time.

"Oh, please don't call me Mr. Harris," the man replied, shaking his head. "I'm just Cody. Always have been, always will be."

"Dad and Cody, this is Izzy and Brooke from my school, and Izzy's brother, Zack—and his penguin," said Tai.

"How thoughtful of you to bring a penguin," Cody said, smiling at Zack. "We've never had *that* type of bird at any of our banding stations."

Zack looked at his sister with a huge grin.

Mr. Davis checked his watch. "It's time for a net run. You kids ready?"

Izzy, Brooke, and Zack had no idea what a "net run" was, but they nodded and followed.

They walked from net to net checking for birds. The nets were made of black nylon and were hard to see until you walked right up to them. They were strung between two poles so birds would fly right into them. At nets one, two, and three, Mr. Davis yelled, "All clear," so they set off to net four.

"What do you think they'll do if there's a bird in one of the nets?" Izzy whispered to Zack as they walked along.

"I dunno. Will you ask?" he whispered back.

"Uh . . . ," Izzy said, trying to get either Mr. Davis's or Cody's attention, but neither of them heard her, so she looked at Zack and shrugged.

"Why are you catching birds?" Brooke asked brightly as she skipped up to walk with Mr. Davis.

"We want to know if there are the same number of birds from one year to the next," Tai's dad replied.

Izzy was puzzled. How would they know? She

was really curious but just couldn't ask.

Luckily, Brooke had no trouble. "How do you know how many there are?" she asked.

"We count the birds each year and compare our results over time," he answered. "If the numbers are going down, we want to know why."

"What would make the numbers of birds go down?" Brooke asked. Izzy listened eagerly for the answer.

"Well, if there are fewer young birds, we guess the problem lies here, where the birds make nests and have young. If there are fewer adult birds, then it's likely there's a problem where the birds spend their winters, which can be thousands of miles from here."

This reminded Izzy about what Miguel had said about some birds flying south from California to Nicaragua for the winter.

As they arrived at the fourth net, Mr. Davis's eyes lit up. In the net were four birds.

Izzy realized the net was close to where she had seen the bright-yellow bird and the nest. One of the birds tangled in the net was a dull yellow color. *What if it was the little bird I watched hatch?* she wondered.

"I'm going to get out those mountain chickadees first," Mr. Davis said, reaching for two black-and-white birds. "They can get overly tangled if they're in the net too long."

In just moments, he had gently taken the two birds out of the net and slipped them into small cotton bags that he secured with drawstrings.

Izzy breathed a sigh of relief.

"I bet these are a pair," Mr. Davis said. "And look, Cody has a warbling vireo," he added as Cody pulled a gray bird out of the net and slipped it into a bag.

Finally, Cody reached for the dull-yellow bird. "This one is a juvenile Wilson's warbler," he said while removing him from the net. And," he examined the bird, then looked at the kids and smiled, "it's a *Mr.* Wilson because he's a male. When he's grown up, he'll have black feathers on the top of his head, almost like a cap."

"He's amazing," Izzy whispered. "He looks a little bit like some birds I saw at the nest right near this spot."

"He very well might be one of their young," Cody said.

"Maybe it's the bird you watched hatch," Zack whispered.

"That would be incredible," Izzy whispered back to him.

Cody held the bird in a gentle but firm grip so it wouldn't injure itself struggling. Mr. Wilson didn't seem scared but looked around with shiny black eyes.

"If I was going to be one of those birds, I'd be Mr. Wilson, even if it meant I had to be a boy," Brooke said. "He's the only one dressed in a lively, fun color!"

Cody looked down at his worn-out boots and dusty, gray jeans and chuckled. "I guess I'd probably be a vireo."

Once all four birds were in bags, Mr. Davis said, "How 'bout you kids head back to the banding station with Cody while I check the other nets?"

Izzy could hardly wait. Finally, she would get to see what bird banding was all about.

7

The banding station turned out to be a tarp laid out on the grass under the oak tree where they had met earlier.

First, Cody took one of the chickadees out of its bag and examined it, looking closely at its feathers and taking measurements.

"Okay, now, here's the banding part," he said and fastened a tiny metal band to one of the bird's legs with a small pair of pliers. "See, each band has a different number stamped on it," he explained. "That way, we know in the future if we've caught the same bird."

He then opened his hand to let the chickadee fly away. Izzy gasped as it disappeared into the distance. Cody banded the second chickadee and the vireo using the same technique. Finally, he opened the last bag to reach in and gently grab

Mr. Wilson. Mr. Wilson fluttered to get away, but Cody grasped him quickly and held him expertly. "And here is Mr. Wilson," Cody said as he brought out the bird.

"As with the others, I start by figuring out if he's healthy and then by estimating his age," Cody said. He held Mr. Wilson firmly and blew all over his body.

"What are you doing?" asked Izzy, forgetting her shyness.

"I'm blowing his feathers apart to see if he has enough fat on him and to see if he's breeding. I'm also checking the condition of his feathers, and I'm looking at his skull to see if it's fully formed."

"What do you mean?" Zack blurted out. "How could he only have part of a head?"

They all laughed. "Everyone is born with a skull that isn't fully formed," Cody explained. "But that doesn't mean there's only part of a head. It means part of the skull is still soft and needs to solidify. Your skull was the same when you were born." He paused and turned Mr. Wilson over to look at his chest and belly. "If this were an adult bird, I'd also look for a 'brood patch.' Do any of you know what that is?"

Tai nodded. "I do! When a bird's got to keep its eggs warm, it loses some feathers on its belly so its body heat can get right to the eggs."

"That's right," said Cody. He put a metal band on Mr. Wilson's leg and weighed him. When Cody was about to let go of Mr. Wilson, he paused and said, "This little bird will fly all the way to Central America for the winter. My guess would be Nicaragua."

Izzy's eyes grew wide. "My pen pal, Miguel, is from Nicaragua!" she blurted out. "He just told me some birds migrate between there and here."

"That's amazing!" Brooke said. "He must be a tough little bird."

"Um, Cody?" Izzy asked, her face turning a deep red. "Could we call him Señor Wilson, in honor of his migration?"

"Awesome idea!" Brooke chimed in. "Señor Wilson, the migrating warbler."

"Absolutely," agreed Cody. "Would one of you like to release Señor Wilson?"

Izzy started to raise her hand but then saw Zack's eager expression. "Can my little brother do it?" she asked. She didn't feel quite so nervous asking on behalf of her brother.

"Sure thing," agreed Cody. "Zack, your sister is going to have to hold that penguin so it doesn't get jealous."

Zack quickly handed over Otto and reached out to take hold of Señor Wilson.

"Wait a second there, partner," Cody laughed. "Just stand still and hold your hand flat."

Cody put the bird on Zack's palm. Señor Wilson hesitated, but then flew right off.

"I can't believe I held a real bird!" Zack said to Izzy with his eyes wide.

Izzy, Brooke, and Zack stayed until Mr. Davis and Cody had taken down the last net. They had seen more than thirty-seven birds up close, and they had all gotten to release a bird.

It had been an incredible day and none of

them were ready to say goodbye, so the kids wandered around and picked up litter while the adults cleaned up the equipment. When it was finally time to go, Tai asked, "Want to come again next time?"

***

Over the next banding sessions, the kids got in the habit of always picking up litter at the end, and during that time, they got to know each other a lot better.

Tai talked about his horse, Dune, and about training to get his brown belt in karate. He shared that his father had a new girlfriend who seemed nice, but he felt upset sometimes that she was taking the place of his mother.

Brooke told them how she wanted to learn to play softball. She also talked about her older brother, who had left home three years ago to join the Marines. She didn't usually talk about him, because she missed him so much.

Izzy shared that she wanted to bring her mother to the meadow more often but that ever since her father had died, her mother never seemed to have any free time and, worse, never seemed truly happy. Zack picked at the grass and sat close to Izzy while she talked.

For the last few weeks of school, Izzy, Brooke, and Tai ate lunch together every day, and when school got out for the summer, they spent as much time together as possible—often at the banding station. Each time they went, they learned a little more about birds and bird research and a lot about each other.

In addition to banding, Mr. Davis taught the kids other ways to study birds, such as using their songs to identify them and setting up "point count" routes. The kids would stand at each point for five minutes and write down the names of all the birds they heard as well as how many birds there were of each species.

Mr. Davis said they would do the same thing every year to learn whether the number of birds or types of birds at each point changed over time. And if they did change, they would try to figure out why and whether there was anything they could do to help the birds.

Way too quickly, summer was coming to a close and there was only one banding day left. Unfortunately, it was scheduled on the day Izzy's family was moving to Southern California.

"At the very least, you've got to come say goodbye," Tai urged.

Izzy promised they would try.

8

When moving day arrived, Izzy started the morning with a letter to Miguel. She had meant to write it in Spanish this time, but since she was in a rush, she wrote in English again.

Dear Miguel,

You won't believe this, but we're moving today. It's awful. Summer went way too fast! Brooke and Zack and I made a new friend named Tai. He has a horse and is about to get a brown belt in karate. His dad and his dad's friend Cody taught us how to band birds. It's crazy. They catch the birds in these invisible nets and then measure them and put tiny metal bands around their legs.

They taught us a lot about birds. They even taught us about a bird that spends its winter in Nicaragua! It's called a Wilson's warbler and it's yellow. The first one we banded was a baby and might have even been the one I saw hatching—we named him Señor Wilson! I've learned so much this summer. Now I'll be able to understand you better when you write about birds.

I hope you are well and don't have to move. I hope your soccer team is winning.

Your friend,

Izzy

Just as she finished, Izzy heard the moving truck rumble up the driveway. She tucked the letter into her bag and ran downstairs to find her mom, who was showing the movers around. Zack was running around the house gathering up his stuffed animals, Carson was crying from all the commotion, and there was a constant flow of neighbors coming in and out to wish them well.

Then Grandma Pearl stopped by to say goodbye and give each kid a gift for the trip. She gave Carson a stuffed owl that hooted when he hugged it, to keep him entertained on the drive.

Zack got an orange T-shirt because, to Zack, anything orange was good luck. And to Izzy, Grandma Pearl gave her first hockey puck to remind Izzy to be brave. When she left, there wasn't a dry eye among them.

Things were just starting to calm down when Brooke burst into the house, noisy as always. "Izzzzzzzy! Where are you?! I can't believe you're leaving today!" she wailed. "I can't go banding without you."

Izzy's mom sighed. "Izzy, how about if you take Zack and Carson to go banding with Brooke while I work with the movers?"

"Awesome!" Brooke yelled.

Izzy didn't want to leave. It felt unsettling to walk away while strangers packed up all their stuff. She also wasn't too happy about having Carson tag along.

"C'mon, it's no fun sitting around here and watching them pack up all your stuff. Come with me!" Brooke said, pulling Izzy toward the door. And, sure enough, once Izzy was outside and heading toward the park, her mood brightened. When they got to the creek, they spotted Tai following Cody to one of the nets.

"Hey Tai!" Brooke shouted. "Look who's here!"

Tai grinned and waved. "Woohoo!" he hollered.

"I thought my mom would need help packing, but she sent us over here to get out of the way," Izzy explained. "I hope it's okay I brought my little brother Carson along. My mom made me. He's kind of a pain, but it's not his fault. He's only two and a half."

Tai smiled down at the toddler. "I'll bet you're the famous Carson."

Carson stuck his tongue out at Tai and they all laughed.

Mr. Davis was standing at the oak tree with a bird in his hand. "Welcome back," he said. "This here is a three-year-old male black-headed grosbeak. You can tell its age and whether it is male or female by the color and pattern of its feathers."

41

This bird was much bigger than the others they had seen—and much more active. At one point, it got a good bite of Mr. Davis's fingertip.

"Ouchie!" cried Carson.

"That's true, Carson," Mr. Davis agreed while examining his fingertip. "That hurt." He looked down at the kids. "Have you noticed anything different about the birds lately?" he asked.

They stood thinking quietly until Brooke piped up. "You told us about their feathers changing, and I think I've seen that," she said.

"Exactly," said Mr. Davis. "The young birds previously only had fluffy, downy feathers to keep them warm. Now they are growing in feathers that are long and stiff and will allow them to fly. And the older birds are changing out their worn-out feathers for new ones. They're getting ready to fly south for the winter. Anyone know what that journey south is called and why the birds do it?" he asked.

Izzy knew the answer from Miguel's letter, but she held back, twisting her ponytail around her index finger.

"I know, I know!" called Brooke. "It's called 'migrating'! The birds fly south and spend the winter where it's warmer because it gets too cold here. Then they fly back in the spring."

"That's right," said Mr. Davis. "And it's not just their new feathers that tell us they're getting ready. You'll also see their behavior changing. Most birds are gathering into loose groups."

"Flocks!" Zack corrected him.

"Right, flocks," Mr. Davis agreed, smiling. "They'll stay in those flocks to feed on insects together and put on weight for their long flight south." He paused and checked his watch. "It's time for a net run."

9

The kids got to watch three rounds of banding before they saw Izzy's mom walking toward them. "Time to get going," she called. When she caught up to them, she scooped up Carson and held him close. Izzy noticed that her mother looked even more tired than usual.

Mr. Davis quickly stuck out his hand. "You must be Mrs. Philips," he said. "I'm Dustin Davis, Tai's father. Your kids have been terrific helpers this summer."

Izzy's mom shook his hand. "The kids loved it. Thank you for all you've done for them."

She turned to Izzy and Zack. "Kids, the moving truck is ready and it's time for us to go."

Right then, Cody walked up, carrying a cotton bag from the last net run. "Greetings," he said to Mrs. Philips.

Mr. Davis quickly jumped in. "Mrs. Philips, I'd like to introduce you to Cody Harris, my research partner."

"It's a pleasure to meet you," said Mrs. Philips. "And please, call me Scarlet."

"The pleasure is all mine," said Cody, giving a silly little bow. "Your kids are a lot of fun. I've also enjoyed getting to know your grandson, Otto the penguin." He straightened, noticing her tired but lovely smile.

"Are you and your husband excited about the move, Scarlet?" Cody asked.

Mrs. Philips twisted her wedding ring and quietly answered, "It's just the kids and me. My husband passed away two years ago."

"I'm sorry to hear that," Cody said. He hesitated and then asked tentatively, "Would you have time to see one bird up close?"

Izzy looked at her mom and mouthed, "Please?"

"Okay," Mrs. Philips said. "Just one."

Cody grinned and pulled a yellow bird out of

the bag. "Surprise!" he said to the kids.

"Señor Wilson? Is it really you?" Brooke asked the bird.

"It is indeed," Cody said. "I checked the band number to be sure."

"Mom, this is the bird I told you about!" Izzy said with a broad smile. She noticed he was now yellowish-green on top, with a purer yellow below. But he still had the same shiny black eyes that darted curiously about. And now he had a hint of black feathers on his head too.

"Scarlet, I would like to introduce you to Señor Wilson. We captured him the very first day your kids came banding," Cody explained. "Since he already has a band on his leg, I just have to write down the band number, check him over, and let him go."

Mr. Davis came over to take a look. "Welcome back, Señor Wilson," he said. "Want to show the kids your new flight feathers?"

"Great idea, Dustin," Cody said. He gave everyone a good look at the yellow bird, spreading out the new flight feathers on his wings and tail.

Cody asked Mrs. Philips if she'd like to be the one to let him go. She was reluctant at first, but after some prodding handed Carson to Izzy. Cody took her hand and showed her how to hold it flat. Then he placed the bird gently on her palm.

"Oh! He's so sweet," she said. Señor Wilson hesitated for just a moment before taking off to join his flock. He flew right over Izzy and Carson, dropping something wet on Carson's head.

"Rain!" giggled Carson.

Zack looked down at Carson's head. "Nope. Poop."

The group laughed until their stomachs hurt—even Izzy's mom. "I suppose everyone is a little nervous before taking flight," she said, wiping away tears of laughter. "Thank you. It's great to take a break in the beauty of nature in the middle of a stressful day."

Everyone said goodbye and promised to keep in touch. Izzy and Brooke held hands the whole way back to the house. Over a tearful farewell, they pinkie-promised to remain best friends forever. Then the Philips family got into their car and led the moving truck out of their beloved neighborhood and toward their new home.

10

Eight hours of driving broken up by one hotel room later, the Philips family pulled into their new driveway. Unlike their old house, which had been on a cul-de-sac with a big yard next to Green County Park, their new home was on the second floor of a duplex on a busy street, with no yard and no park. And, unlike in their old neighborhood, where old friends had come over to give them a warm send-off, in their new neighborhood, no one stepped outside to greet them or offer help.

As the movers unpacked the truck, Izzy asked her mom, "Can Zack and I go explore the neighborhood?"

Mrs. Philips took a deep breath and sat the kids down together before answering. "Kids, there are more cars here, and lots of strangers. I don't want you going outside without me, and right now I need to stay inside and unpack."

Izzy started to protest, but her mother was firm. "I need you to work with me, Izzy, not add to my worries. Why don't you start unpacking in your room?"

Izzy felt tears well up. Not add to her mom's worries? As if Izzy didn't have plenty of her own! She grabbed her suitcase and pulled it toward the room she would be sharing with Zack. It was dark and small, a big change from the sunny room she'd had all to herself back home. She opened her suitcase and pulled out her framed photos of Brooke and Grandma Pearl, which she'd carefully laid on top, and placed them on her bedside table. "Be brave, be brave," she whispered to herself.

Mrs. Philips worked straight through the afternoon, finally stopping to look for the uniforms and school supplies the kids would need to start school the next day.

"Mom, I'm hungry!" Zack complained.

Mrs. Philips stopped, looked at the mess

around her, and sighed. "Anyone for pizza?"

"Yay!" yelled the kids.

After eating at the local pizzeria, they picked up groceries on the way home. When they got back, they piled onto their mom's bed and watched a movie. Izzy was so exhausted, she forgot to even worry about starting school the next day as they all fell into a deep sleep.

***

"Rise and shine!" Mrs. Philips called out as she pulled open the curtains. "Time to put on those cute new uniforms and have some French toast."

Izzy hardly spoke as she put on her uniform, a blue button-down shirt and plaid skirt with matching blue knee socks. She'd never had a school uniform before. She imagined Brooke wearing something new and colorful for her first day of fifth grade.

Zack put on his uniform, too—a green version of the same outfit, but with plaid shorts—and then set up a line of stuffed animals with Otto in the middle.

"Zack, why are you taking all your animals out?" Izzy asked with a groan. "We're supposed to be getting ready for school."

"I don't want Otto to be lonely while I'm at school," Zack explained.

At breakfast, Izzy could hardly eat, but Zack gobbled his food and even finished Izzy's. He packed, unpacked, and repacked his backpack with his new crayons, pencils, and glue, while Izzy stared out the kitchen window at the busy street. Instead of the meadow, trees, and blue sky she was used to at home, she saw only cars, a parking lot, and closely packed houses. At least there was a large juniper tree right out front, where there might be birds to watch.

Then it was time to go. They piled into the car, and Mrs. Philips drove them to their new school.

11

Izzy had hoped to arrive early and take a look around before starting her first day, but the Philipses arrived just as the bell rang. Since her mom was taking Zack to meet his teacher, Izzy was on her own.

Timidly, she entered her classroom and counted twenty-eight kids—a much bigger class than she was used to, and, somehow, the kids seemed older. Everyone wore the same uniform, but there was a group of girls near the front of the class wearing matching striped socks and blue sneakers. They were talking and laughing loudly together.

When the teacher walked in and called the class to order, Izzy looked down at her white knee socks and loafers and crept to the back of the room to take a seat. Izzy shrank into her seat when Ms. Fox introduced her, along with a few other new students, and for the rest of the morning she did her best to be invisible.

At lunch, Izzy walked to the cafeteria behind the rest of the class. She scanned the room and saw the same group of girls in their matching socks and shoes sitting together. To get to the back of the cafeteria, she had to pass them, so she walked quickly, with her head down.

As she walked by she heard one of them say, "Back handsprings are too easy. Let's get right to flips tonight at gymnastics."

Izzy got her lunch and rushed to a corner table to sit by herself. She lowered her face over her untouched food so no one could see her tears. How was she ever going to make friends here?

After lunch, the afternoon dragged slowly. It was hard for Izzy to listen to her teacher when all she could think about were Brooke and Tai. She pictured Grandma Pearl and had to wipe away more tears.

She snapped out of her daydream as Ms. Fox

announced, "This spring, each of you will make a speech about an activity you enjoy, so I want you to start thinking of your topic now." Izzy could feel a knot form in her stomach. Give a speech? She twisted her hair so tightly her scalp tingled.

Finally, the bell rang. Izzy followed the other kids out of the building and stood alone at the flagpole to wait for her mom. Thankfully, Mrs. Philips showed up quickly, holding Zack's hand. He was talking excitedly about his day, and Mrs. Philips didn't have a chance to ask Izzy about hers before they set off to collect Carson from daycare. He'd had a good day, too.

Back in their new home, Mrs. Philips hung artwork from Zack's first school day on the fridge. She poured three glasses of lemonade and one cup of milk, pulled Carson onto her lap, and asked the kids to come sit by the front window where they could see the juniper tree.

"Let's do our roses and thorns," she said. "Tell me, what were the best parts of your day? And did you have any challenges?"

"I'll start!" Zack shouted. "My roses were my new teacher and my new friends, and I didn't have any thorns."

Mrs. Philips smiled and squeezed Zack's hand, then turned to Izzy with a questioning look.

Izzy shook her head. "You can go next, Mom," she said, looking down to hide her tears.

"Okay," Mrs. Philips said. "I had two roses today: picking all of you up at the end of the day and finding out I have a nice office with great coworkers. My thorn was getting a parking ticket!"

"Oh no, Mommy! Are you going to jail?" Zack cried in a panic.

Izzy laughed for the first time that day. "You don't go to jail for a parking ticket, silly. You just pay a fine."

"Are you sure?" asked Zack.

"Yes," Izzy and Mrs. Philips said together.

"Okay, Izzy," said Mrs. Philips, turning to her. "What are your roses and thorns?"

"Oh, Mom," Izzy said as her tears spilled over.

"I miss Brooke and Tai and Grandma Pearl and our house and the park. I want to go back."

"Honey, don't worry. You'll make friends. How about if we sign you up for gymnastics tomorrow?"

"Gymnastics?" That was the last straw for Izzy. Tears rolled down her cheeks. "Mom, I can't even do a back handspring and these girls at school are already doing flips!"

Izzy's mom wiped her tears and hugged her. "Izzy, I love you so much. I promise things will get better. Moving here is a big adventure for us, and we are only at the beginning."

Only at the beginning. That was exactly what Izzy was afraid of. Izzy's mom tucked her into bed that night and made her feel loved, but long after her mother left the room, she lay awake, holding onto the hockey puck her grandmother had given her. "I am stronger than I think," she whispered to herself. "Be brave."

12

Back at Green County Park, the birds that would fly south for winter grew restless. The long, hot days of summer were drawing to a close; the winds were shifting, the nights were getting colder, and the birds were starting their migrations. Some birds left on their own and others left in flocks. At the same time, birds were arriving in Green County Park from places farther north. They stayed for a day or two to feed and rest before continuing south.

Señor Wilson was also ready to fly south. After days of continual eating, fat bulged from his throat. In fact, he had doubled his weight with stores of fat that would fuel his journey. He had also grown new feathers for his flight. They were duller than the bright-yellow feathers of his parents, but they were strong.

Then one day, his parents left. A few days later, two of his sisters and a brother left. The next afternoon, when a cold front moved in, the birds around Señor Wilson took off one by one—and he took to the air as well. He didn't know how far he would fly or how long he would be gone, but he wasn't turning back. This was it!

Señor Wilson and the other birds in his flock flew for hours upon hours, often silently but occasionally calling to each other. They flew all night every night, stopping at dawn to spend the day resting and feeding in woody thickets and forests. On clear nights, Señor Wilson flew high in the sky and used the stars to guide his way.

When visibility was poor, he flew below the clouds and used the landscape for orientation. Mostly, though, he used the pull of the magnetic fields that run along the earth.

As Señor Wilson flew, he grew stronger and more aware of the risks of the journey. He learned to avoid power lines and tall buildings. One night he became confused by the bright lights of a city but managed to get back on track. There was also the constant risk of going hungry. Often the birds flew over great sprawls of buildings, with no place to rest and eat.

Even worse, on their second day out, Señor Wilson and many of his group were grounded by an unexpected late-summer storm. Some of the birds huddled together for warmth and others found safe places to wait it out. The storm continued for two whole days. The birds were all hungry and cold. As the hours dragged on, they were in real danger of starving.

But late the following afternoon, the skies cleared. Señor Wilson took off into the night, a brilliant map of stars before him. The next morning, he looked for a place to rest and feed on insects. He passed over highways and shopping malls and even an airport, but there were no undeveloped areas for him to land. Eventually, he spotted a big juniper tree, right in the middle of the city.

13

As late summer turned to fall, Izzy struggled to adjust to her new life. Her mom brought home a dark-gray cat, thinking a new pet might help. Izzy and her brothers loved the cat. Zack named him Shadow. But it didn't help Izzy shake the feeling that everything in her life was going wrong.

She didn't have any friends. She didn't even know how to *make* friends. She had barely said a word at school. And she really didn't want to give that speech at school next spring, in front of all the other kids. Every night, she gazed at the photos of Brooke and Grandma Pearl and reminded herself to "be brave," but it didn't seem to be helping.

She also felt like a prisoner in her own home. In their old neighborhood, she and Zack could play outside as long as they were back in time for dinner. Here, she always had to be within her mother's sight. One Saturday morning, however, Mrs. Philips said that she'd become more comfortable in their new neighborhood and would let the kids play outside without her as long as they stayed right in front of the house.

Izzy and Zack were so excited they grabbed a ball and burst out the door in their pajamas. As Izzy looked up to the sun, smiling for what felt like the first time in weeks, she heard laughter and turned to see three of the girls with the striped socks from her class walking down the sidewalk toward her. Izzy froze. She was in her pajamas! Before she could think, the girls were in front of her house. "Um . . . hi," stammered Izzy. "Um . . . going for a . . . walk?"

The girls stopped talking and looked at Izzy curiously. Izzy looked down at her old, faded pajamas and felt her insides crumble. By the time one of the girls asked, "You're new, right?" a wave of panic was already running through her body. Rather than answer, she turned and ran back into the house, slamming her bedroom door and throwing herself on her bed. "I hate this place!" she sobbed into her pillow. "I want to go home!"

Zack and Mrs. Philips rushed into the room. "What is it? What's happened?" Mrs. Philips asked. When Zack filled their mom in, she gathered Izzy into her arms. "It will be okay, honey," she soothed. "Those girls don't care if you were in your pajamas. And if they do, they're not the type of friends you want. You'll make new friends soon."

Izzy kept sobbing into her pillow. *Her mom had no idea how hard it was for her here*, she thought. *And now she would be the running joke at school! Those girls were probably laughing about her even now*. "I just need a little time alone," she sniffed.

Mrs. Philips gently moved a strand of hair from Izzy's tear-stained cheek. "Okay. But we'll be right here if you want to talk."

Alone in the room, Izzy cried until her tears ran out, then she fell into a deep sleep.

When she opened her eyes an hour later, she sat up, took a deep breath, and looked at the photos of Grandma Pearl and Brooke. "I'm stronger than I think," Izzy repeated to herself. She got dressed in her standard jeans and T-shirt but added a Brooke-inspired sparkly headband. Then she called out to Zack. "I'm ready to go back outside, are you?"

Zack appeared immediately with Shadow in his arms. "I'm ready," he answered.

They stepped out and Izzy checked the mailbox. Rewarded with a letter from Miguel, she sat down on the front steps to read it while Zack and Carson played with Shadow nearby.

Querida Izzy,

How is your new home? Have you made any friends? I can't wait until Señor Wilson gets here. I watch for him every day. This is a great place for birds to spend the winter. It is also a great place for people. My father makes delicious fried plantains and roasted corn, not to mention the best gallo pinto—or rice and beans—in town. Maybe you will visit one day—or even come here to live! Why don't you join a soccer team to make friends? I've made many friends playing soccer.

Saludos,

Miguel

14

Izzy was wondering if there was a sport she'd be brave enough to play when she heard a loud *thud*. Izzy looked up, but nothing seemed out of place, so she put her head back down to reread the letter from Miguel.

But then Shadow pounced on something near the building.

Izzy and Zack rushed over and saw it was a yellow bird! They shouted at the cat, who dropped the bird and ran off. Unfortunately, Carson was closer.

"Birdie!" he yelled and snatched up the bird in his pudgy hand.

"No, Carson!" Izzy shouted and took it from him. Ignoring Carson's cries of protest, she said, "I think this bird must have flown right into our window before being picked up by Shadow." Then she started to examine it. "Zack, he's a Wilson's warbler," Izzy said. "And he has a band! Do you think he could be Señor Wilson?"

"That would be amazing," said Zack.

"Unless . . . ," Izzy said, fighting tears as she looked at his injury.

"Unless what?" Zack asked. "He's going to be okay, right?"

Izzy took a deep breath and let it out slowly before forcing a smile. "I'm sure he'll be fine."

Izzy showed the bird to Zack and then leaned down to let Carson have a closer look. Carson pointed to the bird and said "Owie!" He was right. The bird had a small injury on his right wing.

"Let's go inside so I can make a hospital box for him," Izzy said.

The kids went back inside and then Izzy gently handed the bird to Zack. She instructed him to keep the bird safe while she prepared a cardboard box where the bird could rest and recover. She also grabbed a pencil and paper.

"Zack, before you put him in the box, tell me

the band number. I'll write it down so we can ask Tai's dad and Cody if they banded it. Then we'll know if it's Señor Wilson."

Izzy's heart beat quickly as she wrote down the number. Then, while Zack gently put the bird in the box, Izzy asked her mom to call Tai's dad and tell him the band number.

Izzy and Zack hovered while their mom talked to Mr. Davis. She finally gave him the band number but then said, "Sure, I'd love to speak with Cody, if it won't hold up your barbecue."

"Mom, what about the band?" Izzy whispered urgently, but Mrs. Philips ignored her and stayed on the phone.

While they waited, Izzy left to check on the bird and was relieved to see him flutter his wings when she peered into the box. When she returned, Zack was jumping around, desperately wanting to hear about the band. Izzy was also anxious but liked watching her mom smile and laugh as she talked to Cody. It reminded her of the way her mother used to smile when her dad was alive.

Finally, Mrs. Philips asked Izzy if she wanted to talk to Tai. "Yes!" Izzy said and reached for the phone.

"Put it on speaker!" Zack demanded.

Izzy pushed the speaker button, and Zack sat next to her to listen.

"Tai, we miss you," Izzy started.

"I miss you, too," Tai said.

"Did your dad look up the band number?" Izzy asked eagerly.

"He did! You aren't going to believe this," Tai said. "That bird at your house *is* Señor Wilson! My dad said he's on his way to Central America!"

"No way!" Izzy shouted. She and Zack looked at each other in amazement. Then Izzy whispered to herself, "Okay, Senor, you have to be okay," and took a deep breath before turning back to hear more about her friends back in Green County.

Tai updated them on everything from what he was learning in karate to his father's research on golden eagles, to the latest field trip at school. He also said Brooke's brother had come home for a long visit and was teaching her to play softball. Then it was Izzy's turn. She told Tai all about what had happened with the girls that morning, and about their house and their school, and made him promise to tell Brooke she missed her.

While Señor Wilson rested in the box in their living room, Izzy read more about Wilson's warblers in her bird book. She learned they were named after a Scottish poet named Alexander Wilson, who immigrated to the United States. In the U.S., he became a teacher and wrote a series of books about birds. Izzy also read that Wilson's warblers spend their winters in Central America, just as Tai's dad had said.

After dinner, Izzy peeked in again at Señor Wilson. His wing looked a lot better. Was he healthy enough to migrate? Izzy wasn't sure but decided it was time to set him free. She and Zack locked Shadow inside and then took the box outside. When they took off the lid, at first, Señor Wilson didn't move from the safety of the box.

Then Carson reached for him. The toddler's hand was all it took to get Señor Wilson moving. In moments, he was out of the box and flying away.

After Izzy watched the yellow bird fly off, she wrote to Miguel about the whole incident. She knew his mother had made huge efforts in the past to save birds in Nicaragua.

Dear Miguel,

Today an amazing and an awful thing happened. The amazing thing was that Señor Wilson visited us on his way south! The awful thing was that it happened when he banged into our front window. Then our new cat picked him up, and then my little brother grabbed him! We put him in a box to recover and he later flew off, but I'm so worried about him. I wonder if he'll be okay? And how do I keep the same thing from happening to other birds? I don't have any friends yet and I miss my old home.

Your friend,

Izzy

15

While Izzy was writing her letter, Señor Wilson found a secluded spot in a tree down the street to eat, rest, and recover until nightfall. By the time it was dark, he was strong enough to start flying south again. He flew over mountains and rivers, deserts and prairies. He flew over children playing outside and adults drinking coffee.

He flew out of the United States and into Mexico, over Guatemala and Honduras, and into Nicaragua. Finally, in late September, Señor Wilson flew into a town called Ticuantepe and landed at the edge of a small coffee *finca*, or farm, called Finca Verde, to spend the winter.

16

One afternoon in early fall, Miguel was playing soccer in his hometown of Ticuantepe, Nicaragua. The score was two to two with just one minute left in the game. One of the players on the other team, the *Halcónes*, or Falcons, had the ball. She dribbled it right around the Tiburones midfielder and passed it to her teammate to take a shot at the goal.

Miguel sprinted up to him, stole the ball, and made a perfect pass to one of his teammates. That player made a shot at their goal. He missed, but the ball bounced off the goalie's foot and another teammate kicked it in! The game ended, three to two. The Tiburones had won again.

Miguel walked home feeling great. On his way, he checked the mail and found a letter from Izzy. He shoved the letter into his backpack and ran into the house. Izzy and Miguel knew how to use email, but they both loved getting handwritten letters. As soon as Miguel got inside, he ripped open the envelope and began reading.

"Oh no!" he exclaimed as his mother walked into the room.

"*Qué pasó, hijo mío*?" she asked.

"I'm reading a letter from Izzy. A bird crashed into their window and fell to the ground. Then her cat grabbed the bird, and then her little brother grabbed the bird from the cat! The bird is okay. But she wants to know what to do to keep it from happening again."

"Miguel, you know what she should do. I know because I taught you myself," his mother said. "Just tell her."

"Will she think I'm mad at her for letting it happen?"

"Not if you say it with kindness. She wants to know how to help the birds, and you should tell her. Now, let's eat dinner and then get you ready for bed."

When Miguel's mother tucked him in that night, he asked her to tell him the story about how she had saved the birds at Finca Verde, the farm where she and Miguel's dad had worked for the past twenty years.

"Well, let me think, Mijo," she said. "It happened over fifteen years ago—before you were born. Carlos, my boss, wanted to grow bigger coffee plants, so he cut down some of the tall trees to give the plants more sun and sprayed chemicals to keep the insects off the plants."

Miguel shook his head side to side and frowned.

"We know that was wrong, but remember," said his mother, "Carlos thought he was doing the right thing." She paused. "I was out in the field when he sprayed the chemicals, and a few days later, I got really sick. I thought I might die."

Miguel hugged his mother. "How did you get better?"

"I laid in bed for a full week before coming back to work. Then Carlos asked me to take it easy and rest every afternoon on the office porch."

"That's when you saw the birds were gone, right?" asked Miguel.

"That's right. I noticed there were fewer birds than there had been before I got sick. I figured they were probably either killed by the chemicals or they had to go somewhere else to find insects. And I also noticed how quiet it was. The howler monkeys were gone, too. I realized it was because they had lost the shade trees they needed."

"But then you were brave, right?"

"That's how your father tells it!" she said, laughing. "I was scared I'd lose my job if I spoke up, but I was even more scared I might die from chemical poisoning if I didn't. So, I told Carlos what I'd observed. It turned out he'd been sick, too, so he was interested in what I had to say."

"And that's when you were the hero!" Miguel said.

"And that's when we worked together to find a solution," she corrected him. "Carlos asked the workers to come up with a plan to sell more coffee without using chemicals, and to protect the rest of the shade trees, too. We did, and it worked. We advertised Finca Verde as an organic wildlife-friendly finca and his business grew and Carlos gave everyone a raise—"

"And he gave you a promotion!" Miguel finished for her.

"Yes, he did. Now you go to sleep so you can come to the finca tomorrow." Miguel's mother kissed him on the cheek and left him to his dreams.

The next morning, Miguel went to the farm with his parents to keep them company while they worked. He brought his binoculars and his journal so he could take notes and make sketches of the birds.

He loved all the birds, but now his favorite was the Wilson's warbler because of its connection to Izzy. One of the warblers by the creek wore a metal band, like the one Izzy had told him about. It even seemed to have an injury on its wing like the one that hit Izzy's window.

"Are you Señor Wilson?" he asked.

When the afternoon faded, Miguel wandered back to the finca's office to wait for his parents. While he waited, he wrote Izzy:

Querida Izzy,

You will never believe this, but I think Señor Wilson is here! I found a Wilson's warbler with a band around his leg and a hurt wing. If it really is him, he is a strong little bird!

And speaking of birds—you are a good person to want to save birds. Here are some things you can do to keep them safe:

First, you can keep birds from hitting the window by making sure they don't see the reflection of the bushes in the window. One way to do that is by moving the bushes away from the window. Or you can add a pattern to the window that the birds will see. Or you can put something up near the window that scares them—like a fake owl or a picture of an owl.

Another thing you can do is to keep your cat

inside. If that isn't possible, only let your cat outside while you are with it and put a collar with warning bells around its neck.

Also, be sure to tell your friends to never use slingshots around birds! I see way too many birds hurt by slingshots around here.

You will feel so good about doing these things for birds. As my mom always says, talk is fine, but action is what makes a difference. You will also feel better if you do something for yourself. Did you start playing sports or start a new hobby to help make new friends?

Saludos,

Miguel

Just as he finished, he saw his parents heading toward him. Miguel added his letter to the pile of outgoing mail in the office and ran down the path the meet them.

17

A week later, Izzy reached into her mailbox and pulled out Miguel's letter. She sat on the front steps and ripped it open. Her mouth fell open when she read about Señor Wilson. Could it possibly be him? Izzy ran inside to share the news with Zack, and the two of them jumped up and down in excitement.

Then she sat back down to reread Miguel's suggestions and resolved to give them *all* a try. She would take action to help birds—and to help herself. She also realized that even if Miguel, Brooke, and Tai weren't with her, she knew she still had their support. And she had the support and love of her family. She would be okay.

That evening after dinner, Izzy told her mom and Zack about Miguel's ideas.

"I want to help!" Zack said, jumping up.

"Yes," Mrs. Philips added, looking down at the contented cat on her lap. "Let's be part of the solution instead of the problem. How about we start with the window?"

"Okay. How do we do it?" Izzy asked.

"Moving the bushes is a good idea, but since we're only renting, I can't do that right away," Mrs. Philips said. She thought a minute and added, "How about if you kids make cardboard cutouts of owls and tape them to the window while I research a longer-term solution?"

That was all it took to mobilize Izzy and Zack. They pulled out cardboard and scissors and got to work. Meanwhile, their mother turned to the Internet. She found many potential ideas but told the kids her favorite one. "We can add colored dots to the window so birds can see it."

"Yay! We get to have a polka-dot window!" Zack said.

"Can they be purple dots?" Izzy asked. "Purple is Brooke's favorite color."

"I don't see why not," her mom answered.

"Especially if it makes you happy thinking of Brooke. I'll order a collar with bells for Shadow, too, so he can still go outside."

"Can't we just keep him inside?" asked Izzy.

"How about a compromise?" suggested her mother. "We can keep him inside most of the time but let him outside when he is wearing the collar and we are with him."

Later that night, Izzy lay in the dark, thinking about what Miguel had written at the end of his letter. Ever since the Pajama Incident, she'd avoided the striped-sock girls at school, keeping her head down and hurrying past whenever she saw them. How long could she keep that up? Maybe it was time to take action to help herself. She slipped out of bed and tiptoed into the bright living room. "Mom?" she said quietly.

"Yes, honey?" Mrs. Philips looked up from her book. "Why aren't you asleep?"

"There's something else," Izzy added tentatively. "I think I'd like to try a new hobby. Can I try karate?"

Her mother couldn't hide her relief. "Let's sign up tomorrow," she said.

"Can I do it, too?" piped in Zack. He had crept up behind Izzy to see what was happening.

"Sure," Mrs. Philips said with a smile. "Now, back to bed, both of you."

18

The next day, the whole family piled into the car and drove to the local karate school. Izzy stood hiding behind her mother, but a dark-haired man at the desk leaned to one side so he could see her and smiled a big welcome.

"Hello. I'm Master Akito. Are you here to join karate?" he asked.

Izzy just stared, so her mom answered, "My daughter, Izzy, and my son, Zack, would like to join."

"Excellent," Master Akito replied. He looked down at Carson. "I suppose this little guy isn't quite ready."

"Not today. But don't they just grow up so fast?" Mrs. Philips sighed.

"They sure do," he replied. Then he turned to Izzy and Zack. "We have a class starting in about twenty minutes with my partner, Master Angie. Would you two like to give it a try?"

"Yes!" Zack shouted.

Izzy kept staring at her shoes, then let her eyes flicker up to Master Akito. "Okay," she mumbled, immediately looking back down and clearing her throat.

As they waited, kids of all ages started filling the room. They wore matching outfits and brightly colored belts. One girl with long blonde hair and a red belt was standing right in front of them. Izzy recognized her as a girl in her class.

"Hi," said the girl. "Are you joining karate?"

"I think so," Izzy mumbled.

The girl smiled. "Great! If you want, you can stand next to me. My name is Erika."

Izzy hesitated, but when the students filed onto the mat, she grabbed Zack's hand and followed Erika.

The class began by working on some of the same karate moves Izzy had seen Tai practicing. Whenever Master Angie asked the group to do something, they answered together with "Yes, ma'am!"

At first, Izzy mouthed it without making a sound, but then Master Angie looked right at her and said, "I can't hear you!"

"Yes, ma'am," Izzy said a little louder.

"I still can't hear you," Master Angie said.

"Yes, ma'am!" Izzy said louder still. Then she bit her lip and looked at Master Angie, waiting for her response.

"That's more like it," Angie said, smiling at her. "Welcome to karate."

Izzy looked over at her mom and smiled.

Toward the end of class, they did sit-ups, push-ups, and even splits. Master Angie then announced they would do tumbling for the last fifteen minutes of class. Izzy joined in as eagerly as all the other students when they got to practice back handsprings.

At school the next day, Erika asked Izzy to sit with her at lunch. Izzy took a deep breath and sat down, wondering what they would talk about. At first, they talked only about karate, but soon they realized they had many things in common, including being bookworms, loving baking, and having two-year-old brothers.

As they talked, Izzy felt happier and more confident than she had in a long time. When lunch ended, she and Erika walked past the group of striped-sock girls. Instead of avoiding them, Izzy took a deep breath and then smiled and waved, and to her surprise, they smiled and waved right back.

As the winter wore on, Izzy and Erika became good friends. Erika helped Izzy and Zack get to the orange-belt rank in karate, and Izzy taught Erika about the local birds. One night, Izzy went to bed and realized that it had been weeks since she'd had to hold the hockey puck from her grandma in order to fall asleep.

Before Izzy knew it, spring had arrived, and the day of her speech loomed closer. She realized she could say quite a bit about karate. She wrote and revised her speech and practiced saying it over and over, but she still dreaded the day she would actually have to stand up and give it.

But Izzy also realized that aside from worrying about her speech, she had been having so much fun at karate and at school that she hadn't written Miguel in months. She sat down at the table by the window and wrote him a letter. And for the first time all year, she wrote it in Spanish. Here is the English translation:

Dear Miguel,

Thank you so much for your last letter. It helped me feel brave. I joined karate and made a good friend. My mom and brother and I worked to fix our window and keep our cat from hurting birds. I am so much happier. Thank you for encouraging me, but I am still terrified to give a speech. Have you seen Señor Wilson lately?

Your friend,

Izzy

19

Meanwhile, Señor Wilson was passing a restful winter at the edge of the finca, where he defended a small territory near a beautiful little creek. He hadn't been able to find an unoccupied territory deeper within the forest— the resident birds that spent their whole lives in Nicaragua had already taken those spots. Those birds had exotic-sounding names like cinnamon-bellied flowerpiercer and turquoise-browed motmot. Still, Señor Wilson thrived in his location. It was safe and moist and shady.

During the day, Señor Wilson spent a lot of time carefully choosing which insects to eat.

Some were poisonous, some had tough shells that couldn't be broken, and some even had sharp points that stabbed you if you tried to bite them. But there were plenty of tasty insects for him to gobble up, which is exactly what he did.

In the evenings, Señor Wilson sat on a branch and listened to the howler monkeys call to each other. They made haunting sounds unlike anything he had heard up north. There were also quieter, more dangerous animals in the forest. One was a snake called a jumping viper. Another was a type of wildcat called a jaguarundi, but Señor Wilson made it through the winter without getting eaten or harmed.

As winter turned to spring, Señor Wilson started to lose his old feathers and grow shiny new yellow ones. His black cap also got bigger and darker.

Each new feather that grew in was tucked inside a little tube of keratin—the same material fingernails are made of—which fell off when the feather was fully grown. Sometimes before the tubes fell off, Señor Wilson would pick them off with his beak, revealing the fully grown, shiny new feather that had grown inside it.

20

Unbeknownst to Señor Wilson, Miguel had been watching him all winter. He admired how this young Wilson's warbler had migrated such a long way, with an injury to its wing. The word *resilience* came to Miguel's mind. It fit the little bird perfectly.

And now Izzy was becoming resilient, too, adapting to her new home. Miguel wanted to find a way to encourage her to stay strong.

Early one morning, Miguel came to the finca with his journal and sat quietly near the creek to wait for the bird. He didn't have to wait long—less than five minutes—before the little bird appeared, now wearing bright-yellow feathers and a black cap. Miguel started sketching him right away. Señor Wilson was not good at sitting still. In fact, he moved almost constantly, but

Miguel worked quickly. He got the basic sketch done before Señor Wilson flew off. Then, while the details were fresh in his memory, he completed the drawing and wrote a single word on the back: *resistencia*, which means "resilience" in English.

After he finished his drawing, Miguel wrote a letter to send with it:

Querida Izzy,

In Central America, some people call warblers like Señor Wilson chipés—pronounced chee-pay, because all the males say is "cheep cheep cheep." But when these same chipés return to the United States, they find their voices and sing beautiful songs to attract females, and that is why you call them warblers. I am sending my drawing of Señor Wilson to you because it is our shared bird. I hope when it gets to you up north, it will help you find your strength—and your voice.

Saludos,

Miguel

Then he carefully folded the drawing and letter, tucked them away in an envelope, and mailed them north.

21

A few days after Miguel sent off the sketch of Señor Wilson, it was time for the real bird to start flying north. For reasons he couldn't explain, Señor Wilson was eager to get back to the meadow where he was born. So, after a few days of restlessness, he took off.

He had already migrated the whole way once, though in the other direction, so this time he was more confident. He knew how to avoid power lines, beware of reflections, and watch for cats. He also had more of an idea about where he could stop to rest. After many days, he arrived safely back at Green County Park.

22

As the letter—and Señor Wilson—were making their way north, a big change was taking place in the Philipses' house. One day in April, Mrs. Philips gathered up the kids to make a big announcement. Right away, Izzy and Zack started guessing what it could be.

"Are you taking us on a vacation?" Izzy asked.

"Are we getting a dog?" piped in Zack.

"Hold on," laughed their mother. "Let me grab Carson so we can sit down together, and I'll tell you together."

Mrs. Philips pulled Carson onto her lap and gathered Izzy and Zack around her. "I'm proud of how you kids have taken to our new life," she said. "You've done well in school and taken up karate. You've both made new friends, too." Izzy and Zack smiled and blushed. "I've done pretty well myself. I've taken on challenges at my new job. And Carson has done great at his daycare." At that, Izzy tickled Carson, who let out a happy squeal. "I think we are going to have a fine life in our new home. But . . . that doesn't mean we have to stay here year round."

Izzy and Zack eyed each other. Izzy asked, "What do you mean? Where are we going?"

Mrs. Philips took a deep breath and continued, "With your Grandma Pearl getting older and having a harder time getting around, I got permission from my boss to work remotely this summer to be near her. I found a house in our old neighborhood that is available for the summer while the owners are away. So . . . I rented it!"

At that, Izzy and Zack went into full celebration mode, dancing and jumping around the house. Izzy's only problem was leaving Erika. But it was only for the summer.

That night, Izzy called Brooke to tell her the good news. "Yippee!" Brooke shouted, and the two chattered about all the fun they would have.

After Izzy hung up the phone, she went outside to check the mail and found a letter from Miguel. Inside, there was a letter, which she read—twice—and a stunning drawing of a Wilson's warbler with bright-yellow feathers and a black cap. Izzy realized Señor Wilson would have his adult feathers by now and wondered if it really could be him. She didn't know Miguel was such a talented artist.

Then she turned the drawing over and, on the back, she found the word Miguel had written: *resistencia*. Izzy looked at the drawing again and thought about how she had changed and grown over the past year, just as Señor Wilson had. With a smile, she tucked the drawing neatly into her backpack, knowing she would need it the next morning at school when she had to stand in front of her class and give her speech.

The next day, when her name was called, Izzy picked up her speech and the drawing and slowly walked to the front of the class. Looking out at the students, she wished the floor would open up and swallow her. But then she took a deep breath, imagined the picture of Señor Wilson with his injured wing, and began her speech.

"My name is Izzy," she said, staring at the floor while a knot tied and untied itself in her stomach. "Today, I am going to tell you about karate." She took a breath and made herself look up at the class.

Everyone was smiling at her! *What?* she thought. *Do they actually want to listen to what I have to say?* She gave them a trembling smile back, took another deep breath, and made it through the whole speech without a hitch.

Afterward, she stumbled back to her seat while everyone clapped. Erika smiled at her, leaned toward her, and gave her a high-five. Izzy smiled back at her. She had done it!

23

Less than two months later, Izzy's family drove north for eight hours and, after stopping at Grandma Pearl's for hugs, arrived at their new summer rental. Izzy and Zack were out of the car the second Mrs. Philips came to a stop. Izzy had told Tai and Brooke they were coming back that day, so they had already made plans to meet at the edge of the meadow.

As soon as they saw each other, they started yelling and running.

"Oh, Izzy, you're back for the whole summer!" Brooke said, jumping up and down. "And you, too, Zack. And Otto!"

"Welcome home," Tai said, grinning.

"We're so happy to be back," Izzy gushed. "We have so much to tell you!"

The friends spent the rest of the afternoon

talking, playing in the creek, and practicing back handsprings, which Izzy could now do with ease.

As Izzy landed her best back handspring yet, she felt something under her foot. Zack kneeled down and pulled a dirty plastic bag off of her shoe. "Yuck!" she exclaimed.

Tai turned serious. "You know how we always pick up litter after a day at the meadow?" Izzy and Zack nodded. "Well," Tai continued, "it's gotten so bad that Brooke and I can't keep up. We even found a bird with a piece of plastic wrapped around its head. It was horrible."

Izzy gasped. "That's awful!" She started to twist her hair and feel sad. Then she remembered what Miguel had told her about taking action. "We love nature and learning about nature. But that isn't enough," she said.

"What do you mean?" Brooke asked.

"My pen pal Miguel says, 'Talk is fine, but action is better,'" Izzy said. "We need to find a way to fix this litter problem."

"How about if we form a nature club for the

summer?" Izzy suggested.

"Yeah! How 'bout we call it, 'The Nature Learning and Action Club!'" Tai said.

That made everyone laugh.

"Too long!" Brooke said. "How about just 'The Nature Club?'"

Everyone agreed on that version.

"And how about if Izzy serves as our first president?" Tai suggested.

"Yes!" said Brooke and Zack in unison.

"I can't be the president," Izzy frowned. "I'm not a leader."

"You're crazy, Izzy," Brooke said. "You'd be perfect. And besides, you have no choice because we voted unanimously."

Izzy wasn't so sure. But she did have an idea about what to do, and she knew she would feel badly later if she didn't go ahead and tell them about it. "Well, okay. Then I suggest we organize a clean-up day for next Saturday morning."

"Excellent!" Brooke agreed. "How about inviting the whole neighborhood? We could make posters to let people know."

"We need a club logo to put on our posters," Tai said.

Izzy snapped her fingers. "I have just what we need!" She unzipped her backpack and pulled out Miguel's drawing of a Wilson's warbler.

"What a great drawing! It looks like . . . ," Brooke shouted.

"What?! Could it be the same bird we banded?" Tai asked.

"The same one you saw hatch out of its egg?" Brooke added.

"It has to be! It's Señor Wilson—all grown up!" Izzy shouted, almost as loudly as Brooke. "And see on the back?"

"*Resistencia.* That's the Spanish word for resistance," Tai said.

"Yes, or resilience. And that's us. We won't give up on nature!" Izzy said.

They walked together to Brooke's house and got to work making posters while Brooke's dad made copies of Miguel's drawing, so they could attach one to each poster. When the posters were ready, the kids headed out on their bikes to hang them all around town.

While they were gone, Brooke's dad called the county parks department to let them know what the kids were planning. The woman who answered the phone was so pleased with the idea that she promised to send over two rangers to bring supplies and help organize the effort.

24

During that week, Señor Wilson was busy, too. As soon as he arrived in Green County Park, he started singing. He sang as he perched in one place, and he kept singing as he flew from perch to perch, marking the boundaries of his territory. Almost right away, a female Wilson's warbler joined him in his territory, built a nest, and starting laying eggs.

25

On Saturday morning, Izzy, Zack, Tai, and Brooke met at Brooke's house to go over their plans one last time, and Brooke's dad came in with a surprise for each of them. He had made them T-shirts that said "The Nature Club" over the picture Miguel had drawn of Señor Wilson. He even had an extra one for them to mail to Miguel. He also gave them each a notebook with the logo printed on the cover so they, like Miguel, could each start a nature journal. They all put on their shirts and marched arm in arm over to the park.

At the park, people were starting to assemble. By nine o'clock, twenty-seven people had arrived, including some kids from school, all of their parents, Mr. Davis's girlfriend, and Cody. Finally, two park rangers arrived and handed out bags and gloves to all the volunteers.

When everyone was ready, the rangers gathered all the participants into a circle and gave a safety talk. Then they introduced the kids as "the Nature Club" and asked them to get the event started. Tai gave Izzy a nudge and whispered, "That would be you, Ms. President."

Izzy stared at the ground, terrified. Speak in front of all these people? It was even scarier than in her classroom. But then she thought about how bravely Señor Wilson had made his way south, even after hurting his wing. And then she thought about all *she* had accomplished over the past year: settling into a new home, making friends, and learning karate.

And she remembered how the other kids had clapped after her speech at her new school. She looked over at her friends, who were cheering her on. She could do it. She stepped forward and, finding her voice, announced, "Thank you all for coming. Let's clean up this park to save the birds!"

Everyone yelled "Hooray!" and off they went. Some groups gathered trash from the creek, others worked around the meadow, and still others cleaned up the parking lot and the road leading into the park.

The plan was for everyone to meet by eleven o'clock at the rangers' truck. As each person or group came back, they threw their bags of trash into the back of the truck. By eleven, there was a huge heap of trash bags and a very satisfied group of volunteers. The rangers assembled all the volunteers in a circle and passed out lemonade.

Mr. Davis gave a short talk about how important Green County Park is for birds. He explained that although some birds live there year-round, others only spend the summers there, and still others only pass through—they all depend on it. He ended by thanking everyone for helping to clean up that important habitat. When he was done, the group cheered.

"You kids are superstars," said one of the rangers in front of everyone. "Thanks for all your help!" At that, the group cheered again, and then everyone left—except the kids from the Nature

Club and their families.

The kids' parents surprised them with a picnic lunch, so they could stay and celebrate. Cody helped Izzy's mom spread two big picnic blankets, and Brooke's parents laid out drinks, fruit, and sandwiches. When everyone had a drink, Tai suggested Izzy make a toast. She blushed but then stepped forward and asked everyone to raise their water bottles.

"To nature!" said Izzy.

"And birds!" said Tai.

"And return migrations!" said Brooke, and they all clinked bottles.

While they ate, Cody told them about the birds he'd seen on vacation in Central America a few years earlier. Izzy couldn't help but notice how her mom's eyes sparkled while Cody was speaking. Tai must have noticed, too, because he looked over at Izzy and winked.

After cleaning up the picnic, the kids took the adults on one last walk through the park, just to be sure every piece of trash was gone. When they were satisfied it was clean, they stopped for a group high five—and accidentally surprised a Wilson's warbler off her nest. Cody gently pulled aside the willows so Mrs. Philips could peer inside. She gasped when she saw there were five perfect eggs.

While everyone took a quick look, Izzy glanced around for the yellow mother. She spotted the bird right away on a nearby branch, impatiently jumping around while waiting for them to leave. But then Izzy spotted another yellow bird a bit farther away.

It looked just like the female, but with a bold black cap, a band on its left leg, and an injured right wing. *Señor Wilson!* she thought. *He had come back!* As soon as the group backed away from the nest so the mother could return, Izzy pointed him out to the group and they all whooped with joy. It was the perfect ending to a fantastic day.

Notes on Wilson's Warblers

by Izzy Philips

Wilson's warblers are also known by their Latin name, *Cardellina pusilla*. They are small, bright-yellow birds with shiny black eyes, rounded wings, and long tails. Their backs are tinted olive, and adult males have black feathers on top of their heads that make them look like they are wearing caps.

Wilson's warblers spend their summers in the United States and Canada, usually in meadows with willows or alders growing next to mountain streams. They migrate to Mexico and Central America for the winter.

The females build nests using leaves, grass, and moss and line them with leaves and hair. Their eggs are creamy white with brown markings. Only the female sits on the eggs, but both parents feed the young.

They move about constantly, grabbing insects or picking them off leaves. Their sweet song is a simple series of short, rapid chips.

✳✳✳

To protect Wilson's warblers and other birds:

- If your windows reflect plants, trees, or flowers, use curtains or window decals to block the reflections and make the window less of a draw to birds.

- Leave fledgling birds where you find them. After leaving the nest, fledglings often spend a few days on the ground until they're ready to fly on their own.

- Protect and restore natural habitat, especially near water sources.

- Keep your distance from birds so you don't disturb them or scare them off of their nests.

- Reduce, reuse, recycle, and pick up litter to protect natural habitats and keep birds from choking on trash.

- Shine outdoor lights down, instead of up into the sky, and turn them off when not in use, so you don't interfere with night-flying birds.

- Keep cats indoors and dogs on leashes so they don't disturb or prey upon birds or their eggs.

- Keep your garden chemical-free so you don't poison birds or other wildlife.

- Keep balloons inside to make sure birds don't swallow pieces of them and choke.

Questions to Consider:

1. Izzy and her friends love Green County Park. Do you have a favorite place?

2. How does Izzy's personality differ from the personalities of her friends?

3. What are some of the challenges Señor Wilson faces during migration?

4. What are some of the challenges Izzy faces when her family moves?

5. What actions does Izzy take to make herself happier in Southern California?

6. What is similar between Izzy's life and Miguel's life, and what is different?

7. How do Izzy and her friends come up with the idea of forming a nature club?

Join the Nature Club for more adventures!

www.natureclubbooks.com

Read on for a peek at Book 2 . . .

Racing with Butterflies
Chapter 1

As Tai rode his horse, Dune, he imagined the outcome of the barrel racing competition at next weekend's Green County Rodeo. *And this year's blue ribbon goes to Tai Davis!*

Tai had won two years in a row in his hometown in Nebraska and then missed last year's rodeo when he moved west with his dad. Dune would soon be too old to race, but, for now, he was strong and fast. *If I win this rodeo*, Tai thought, *I can retire Dune as a local champion.*

Lost in thought, Tai arrived home, unsaddled Dune, and gave him a good brushing. He didn't even hear his father, who had walked out to join him. "How was practice?" Tai's dad asked, handing Dune a bunch of sweet hay.

"I beat my best time," Tai responded with a bit of swagger. "Just a hair under sixteen seconds."

"That's my boy," his dad commended, with a huge grin. "You're going to teach these local cowboys how to ride!"

"I sure hope so—with Dune's help," Tai replied, feeling inside his pocket for his lucky penny. "You know, Izzy and Brooke have never seen a barrel race before. I want to win it with them watching."

Tai released Dune into the pasture while his dad hung his saddle, harness, and tack. When they were done, Tai wiped his brow and leaned against an old cottonwood tree.

He rested for a moment and then broke into a broad grin and jumped into a puddle. As he did, dozens of light-blue butterflies scattered about.

"What're all these butterflies doin'?" Tai asked his dad as he chased them.

"Those butterflies," his dad explained, "are puddling."

"Are what?"

"They're puddling," his dad laughed. "Butterflies gather together and rest on puddles of mud, urine, or even dung to drink water and absorb salts."

"What's dung?" Tai asked.

"You know," his dad responded. "Dung is poop. They don't like the dry, round kind we refer to as 'horse apples'—they're more into the wet, mushed-up kind."

"Oh. Gross," Tai observed.

"I suppose that's true for a human. But butterflies see the world differently," Mr. Davis said. "Come here. I want to show you something you'll like."

They walked to the edge of their pasture and Mr. Davis knelt down. "Take a look at these milkweed plants."

"Why?"

"Because there's a great partnership between milkweeds and one of the most famous butterflies in the land. You can observe it right here if you look closely."

Tai bent down to study a milkweed, and, on it, he saw a large caterpillar banded with black, yellow, and white horizontal stripes. It was busily chewing through a wide, green leaf.

"Oh, good," Mr. Davis said. "You found a monarch caterpillar. Also known by its Latin name, *Danaus plexippus*."

"Dana what?" Tai asked.

"*Danaus plexippus*."

"How about we call her Dana for short?" Tai suggested.

"Fine with me," his father said. "Once Dana goes through metamorphosis, she'll become a beautiful monarch butterfly. You know what metamorphosis is, right?"

"We learned about it in school. It's when something changes form. With butterflies, an egg becomes a larva—and that's the caterpillar. Then the caterpillar becomes a pupa—and that's the chrysalis. And last, the chrysalis becomes an adult—and that's the butterfly."

"Right. In goes a caterpillar and out comes a butterfly," Mr. Davis said.

"Are these monarch eggs?" Tai asked, pointing to tiny green balls on the leaf.

"Oh no. That's frass from your caterpillar,"

answered his dad. "Caterpillar poop," he clarified when he saw Tai's puzzled expression. "The eggs are off-white and tiny. They could fit on the head of a pin." As he talked, he searched a milkweed plant. "Monarchs almost always lay them on the undersides of milkweed leaves. In fact," he paused and pointed to a spot on one of the leaves, "there's one right here. If you look closely, you'll see it's covered in ridges."

Tai examined the egg while his father explained what would happen next. "Within a week, a tiny caterpillar will chew a hole through the egg and work its way out. Then it'll eat and grow continuously—a lot like you these days."

Tai looked up from the egg to make a face at his dad.

Mr. Davis made a face back and continued. "Every few days it will pause to molt—or to shed its skin—so it can keep growing larger until, after about two weeks, it will be over two thousand times bigger than it was when it began."

"Not like me," Tai said.

His dad laughed. "Let's hope. Anyway, each period of time the caterpillar has a new skin is called an 'instar.' Based on Dana's size, banding pattern, and a few other traits, I'm pretty sure she's in her fourth instar.

"The fifth instar is the final one. When she's done growing, she'll find a sheltered spot under a branch to pupate. By pupate, I mean transform into a butterfly. Monarchs do this in an amazing-looking chrysalis. I'll try to find you one . . ." Mr. Davis stopped talking and focused on looking for a chrysalis for a few minutes.

"Hmm. I can't find one right now, but when it finally emerges between one and two weeks later, it'll look like . . ." Mr. Davis looked around, "like that butterfly there," and he pointed to a large, reddish-orange butterfly flying past, with wings that had striking black edges with white dots and a network of black lines within.

They watched the butterfly slowly sail about for a few minutes until it landed on a coneflower.

"I thought you said they only use milkweed,"

Tai said.

"Milkweed is the only plant monarch butterflies lay their eggs on, and once the caterpillars emerge, milkweeds are the only plants they'll eat. Once they are adults, however, they use milkweeds and other plants for nectar."

"Are there a lot of different kinds of milkweeds?" Tai asked.

"I can tell you about butterflies," his dad, who was an expert on all things bird and butterfly said, "but if you want to know more about the plants, you're going to have to ask your mother. She's the best botanist—and the best dentist—I know."

"But she isn't here," Tai said, kicking the dirt with his boot. His parents had separated just over a year ago, right before Tai and his father had moved west. When they had moved, his mother immediately flew to Japan to visit her parents, and since then, had remained in Nebraska. Although Tai had gone back four times to visit her, she hadn't yet come out to Greenley, California, to see where he was living.

"Well, actually," his father said, "I've got a surprise for you."

"Mom's coming?!" Tai asked, his face lighting up.

"She is. She's coming to see you race."

"Next week?" Tai asked, his face now glowing with anticipation.

"She arrives tomorrow and will stay a full week, leaving the following Sunday."

"Awesome! Is she staying with us?" Tai asked hopefully.

"You know that's not realistic," his father answered, "but she'll be right down the street at the Clementine Inn. Now, come on, let's go inside for dinner." Mr. Davis put his arm around his son and they walked to the house together. "It'll be good to see her," he added.

As they entered the house, Tai could smell his dad's specialty, lasagna, and was filled with hope. *My dad is looking forward to seeing my mom,* he thought. *Once they look at each other, they'll remember how much they like each other and . . .*

But then, as he entered the kitchen, Stephanie, his father's girlfriend, walked over. "Hey, Tai," she said, innocently shattering his daydream.

to be continued . . .

Acknowledgments

I am grateful to Wren Sturdevant, Max Sturdevant, John Sturdevant, Elettra Cudignotto, Rachelle Dyer, Allan Mazur, Polly Mazur, Sophie Phillipson, Spencer Phillipson, Kelly Phillipson, Jackie Pascoe, Kim Marcis's elementary school class, Salvadora Morales, Ella Boiano, Binta Wold, Autumn Stock, Lisa Rhudy, Michael Ross, Jennie Goutet, Chuck Carter, Emma Irving, Julie Mazur Tribe, Jenny Mahon, Ceci Jackson, Leslie Paladino, Juan Carlos Macias, Jessica Santina, Sarah Hoggatt, Madelyn Ruffner, and Carol Beidleman for their help and encouragement.

I am also grateful to both Rodney Siegel, executive director of the Institute for Bird Populations, and Salvadora Morales, president of Quetzalli Nicaragua, who generously provided expert review.

About the Author

Rachel Mazur, Ph.D., is the author of *Speaking of Bears* (Globe Pequot, 2015), the award-winning picture book *If You Were a Bear* (Sequoia Natural History Association, 2008), and many articles for scientific and trade publications. She is passionate about writing stories to connect kids with nature—and inspiring them to protect it. Rachel lives with her husband and two children in El Portal, California, where she oversees the wildlife program at Yosemite National Park.

To learn more about The Nature Club series, please visit natureclubbooks.com.

To learn more about the art of Elettra Cudignotto, please visit elettracudignotto.com.

To learn more about the art of Rachelle Dyer, please visit rachellepaintings.com.

Made in United States
North Haven, CT
02 February 2022

15545735R00083